Productivity 21 days Project

Learn how to increase your productivity and efficiency in just 21 days

© **Copyright 2017 By Successdailyread All rights reserved.**

This document is geared towards providing exact and reliable information in regards to the topic and issue covered. The publication is sold with the idea that the publisher is not required to render accounting, officially permitted, or otherwise, qualified services. If advice is necessary, legal or professional, a practiced individual in the profession should be ordered.

From a Declaration of Principles which was accepted and approved equally by a Committee of the American Bar Association and a Committee of Publishers and Associations.

In no way is it legal to reproduce, duplicate, or transmit any part of this document in either electronic means or in printed format. Recording of this publication is strictly prohibited and any storage of this document is not allowed unless with written permission from the publisher. All rights reserved.

The information provided herein is stated to be truthful and consistent, in that any liability, in terms of inattention or otherwise, by any usage or abuse of any policies, processes, or directions contained within is the solitary and utter responsibility of the recipient reader. Under no circumstances will any legal responsibility or blame be held against the publisher for any reparation, damages, or monetary loss due to the information herein, either directly or indirectly.

Respective authors own all copyrights not held by the publisher.

The information herein is offered for informational purposes solely, and is universal as so. The presentation of the information is without contract or any type of guarantee assurance.

The trademarks that are used are without any consent, and the publication of the trademark is without permission or backing by the trademark owner. All trademarks and brands within this book are for clarifying purposes only and are the owned by the owners themselves, not affiliated with this document.

About Us

One of the worst feeling in this world is being incredibly busy but not making any progress and certainly most of us have experienced this at some point of our life. In this challenging century, people need to constantly keep up and expand their knowledge and continually develop new skills to stay relevant and live a meaningful lifestyle. In every book written by our staff at **SuccessDailyRead.com**, we strive to bring you to reveal our key ideas and vast strategies to help you excel in every area of your personal and professional life. You will be given a ticket into the practice and of today's greatest achievers from successful businessmen, revolutionary entrepreneurs and outstanding leaders.

SuccessDailyRead.com is your go-to platform that help our readers to focus and succeed in their own arena. Our reader understands that today world had become more dynamic and the classic way of employer to employee relationship had evolved. No longer could our reader expect a corporate training to remain relevant in their professional field nor expect personal growth without reading and improving. All our readers are solely responsible for their very own growth and should be proactive to find motivation material to achieve their goal.

We believe while others dream of the future, **SuccessDailyRead.com** reader see it built. We believe our reader don't just create business only but they change the world in this revolutionary century. Regardless whether you're a student, a salaried worker, a home maker, an experienced entrepreneur or just starting your business, we hope that you'll never dare to dream and have the courage to make your dreams a reality.

You may be doing well in your life but certainly there's always room for growth and improvement. Our readers are not just here to fix their existing problem or remove any obstacles but they're here to create new possibilities, gain insights on today business challenge, improve their existing life and most importantly "short-cut" their learning curve by years so they can achieve their goals faster.

Bring your goals and take your life and business to the next level TODAY! Subscribe to our newsletter by visiting us at **www.SuccessDailyRead.com**

Let's master our ability to set good habits and positive mindset will have a lasting impact in our life. And we all have it in our power to get started!

Table of Contents

Introduction: Time to change your life 1

Chapter 1: Why do you want to be productive? 5

Chapter 2: How to find your why? 9

Chapter 3: What is the most valuable thing you have? 13

Chapter 4: Letting go: The art of doing one thing at a time..15

Chapter 5: Start off your day right................................18

Chapter 6: 30 minutes morning ritual to bulldoze your day 21

Chapter 7: Avoid Winning lottery mindset...................39

Chapter 8: The need for a break in-between work day 41

Chapter 9: Deadline is not your enemy but your best friend...43

Chapter 10: How to protect your time 45

Chapter 11: The secret to eliminate distractions..........47

Chapter 12: Productivity hacks 50

Chapter 13: Identifying, sand removing your destructive habits 69

Chapter 14: Using your time to your advantage (make it your leverage, not just average!) 72

Chapter 15: Conclusion 75

Introduction: Time to change your life

Hello and welcome to this book. If you are reading this, then it means you have decided to take the steps necessary to overhaul your life and transform yourself. Congratulations on taking this first step and I wish you nothing but success on your journey!

Maybe your days may not tend to go smoothly. You could be good at getting up on time, working your day through and making sure you have sufficient time to relax BUT the problem is you feel that you're not quite adding up altogether.

Starting out is always the hardest part, especially when it comes to transforming your life. Starting might be the hardest part, but it is also the most important part. It brings with it momentum, inspiration, determination and a desire to achieve something.

Those who never start never achieve anything, so take a moment to pat yourself on the back. You've done more than most people ever will in their lives. So, now that you've started- don't stop! The tips and tricks in this book are not just meant to be read, but they are meant to be used and implemented to ensure that you reap the benefits of the suggestions below.

Being productive is not accomplishing more but investing your attention and time in a strategic way to value add your life, career, relationship.

In this book, we will be focusing on a number of different aspects of productivity and using them to maximize your own workflow as quickly as possible. In fact, if you follow the action plan laid out below, you will be on your way to a more productive life within just 21 days. I know 21 days does not sound like a lot of time, but I can guarantee you that you can get more than you have ever dreamed possible done in that time.

On a day to day scenario, things may be good but when you gauge yourself from month to month, you may feel you didn't make significant progress

Commitment, determination and motivation are fantastic tools to making sure that you achieve what you have set out to do. After all, this book lays it all out for you, so all you need to do is work through the book's instructions and you will find the success you crave.

In part one of this book, we will cover the core to improving your productivity. We will discuss why you want to be productive and what you are trying to achieve. We will also talk about finding your 'why', your motivation and your drive! I guarantee that part one will get you all fired up to start working on the rest of this book (that's why we put it at part one!). Never underestimate the power of self-motivation.

In part two, we talk about starting your day off right and letting go of expectations. Of course, we all know that starting our day off right can make all the difference when it comes to productivity, and it is vital to make sure that you pay close attention to your routine and how it might be working for you, or against you!

Part three focuses on creating a shift in your mindset and lays out a few key productivity hacks for your work day. In this chapter we focus on the mindset changes that can make or break your productivity. In fact, we recommend taking notes here! Implementing these suggestions can do you a world of good- they certainly help me get through my work day!

Part four is full of productivity hacks that you can start to implement right away to get you moving again. Some of these hacks are simple, others are more complex, but all of them are valuable and very much doable. Implementing one of these tips each day can make a huge difference to your productivity and work.

Part five of this book wraps it all up. In this part of the book, we will be talking about managing the habits that might be working against you. I have had to troubleshoot many of my own destructive habits on the path to productivity, so I hope that this chapter is as helpful for you as it is for me

So, without further ado, here's how to a great 3 weeks' program so let's move on to the rest of the book- happy productivity!

Chapter 1: Why do you want to be productive

Something that people often fail to consider is the reason and motivation that drives them. Often, we want to be productive because that is what society expects from us, or because our boss is heaping us with a workload that we cannot cope with.

We might want to be productive to make sure we impress our co - workers, or to seem like we are busy. These reasons, while valid, are all external reasons. Other external reasons can include things like fame, money and material things. Money might be a legitimate motivator for some people, but it is important to consider whether or not something else is driving you.

If your reason for being productive is a shallow one that does not serve a greater purpose in your life, then there is a good chance that it will simply cease to motivate you, and your productivity will fall by the way-side.

You need to consider, honestly, what is truly driving your desire for productivity. If you need money to support your family, then love for your family, a strong sense of duty and determination might be what is driving you. Or, perhaps you have found yourself in poverty and your drive is the desire to improve yourself.

Maybe you are striving for a promotion because you want to free up hours to spend with loved ones, or perhaps you are juggling study and work, and your drive is the need to improve yourself and your education.

Maybe you want to be more productive so that you only need to work for a few hours, instead of all day. There are many reasons for wanting to boost your productivity, and all of the ones listed above are very valid. Of course, yours, no matter what it is, is just as valid.

What matters is that it drives you on a deeper level, and that you know why you are working hard. Make sure that you know what you are striving to achieve. Only you know what drives you. Only you know what will make you wake up early and work hard. Only you know why you need to be productive.

It doesn't matter what you tell other people. It doesn't even matter if it is true or not. What you tell other people might be the 'right' answer, the answer that you know society expects to hear. But that might not be your real reason. Sometimes the people around you might not understand, or you might not feel comfortable discussing your intimate reasons and thoughts with them. That is okay- remember that it doesn't matter what you tell other people, but it does matter what you tell yourself.

Always be honest with yourself and don't try to lie to yourself, or your productivity will fall as fast as it has risen. Know why you are working hard, and keep it in your heart and in your mind. If you can do this, then you are already half-way there.

Chapter 2: How to find your why?

What we just discussed in the previous chapter is generally referred to as your

'Why'. It is called this, because it is the reason why you get out of bed in the mornings, it is why you work hard at the office, it is why you spend the extra hours studying. It is your motivation, your drive and your reason for wanting to get things done.

Everyone has a different why, but you need to find out what yours is and keep it close to your heart. Before you implement any hacks, tips and tricks to be productive, you need to make sure that you have discovered your why, and that you put it into practice in a big way.

If, however, this is the first time you have ever heard of this, then it might feel confusing at first, and challenging. How to do you find your why, and how do you know when you've found it?

If you have found your why, then it will resonate inside you. It will be a clear, guiding beacon of motivation that will remind you to stay on course, remind you why you are choosing to work instead of play. You will know your why when you find it, and it will stick with you. If you have been honest with yourself, then you will know your why when you find it.

As for how to find it, that can be a bit tricky at first. However, there are several steps that you can take to establish your why. It can be very useful to grab a piece of paper and a pen for this bit, and set aside enough time to think good and hard about each of these questions.

What are your core values?

Do you value honesty? Are you motivated by love, duty or something else? What are the values that you live your life by, and carry with you in your heart? There is a good chance that you have never had to articulate them before, so it can be hard to put names to these feelings, but it can be very helpful to making sure you achieve what you have set out to do.

Also, it can be quite nice seeing your values set out on paper like that.

Remember, again, that this is for your personal use. Don't put down anything that is false, or you think you 'should' value. Be true to yourself, even if it is challenging, and this will be far more of a success.

What do you spend most of your time doing? What would you like to spend your time doing?

This can give you a good indication of where your interests lie and what might be motivating you to continue forward. For example, if you spend all of your time working, but want to spend time with your family, then you have gotten closer to unlocking your motivation (which could be supporting your family better, or freeing up more time to be with them.) This is just an example, so it might differ for you.

You don't need to track the exact minutes you spend on each activity here, but it is good to have a basic idea of where your time is being spent and how you would like to spend it. Write down all of your thoughts and feelings on this topic, and feel free to take your time.

Have a good look at your core values, and where you spend your time, and consider them carefully. Out of these two things, you should be able to narrow down your focus. That is your why. That is why you are working hard.

Focus on this and keep it in the front of your mind and your heart as you move through this book. It is one of the most important tools you have for improving your productivity.

Chapter 3: What is the most valuable thing you have?

What is the most important thing to you? Is money and security important to you? Or is it freedom? Do you value your time or your comfort? What about both?

Consider what is valuable to you and what you are striving for. Perhaps you feel that your family is more valuable to you than your time, and that their security comes first. Perhaps you are seeking to make sure that you have a future that is brighter than your past. It doesn't matter what is valuable to you, what matters is that you know what it is.

Take a good look at your life, and at your past. Who do you want to be, where are you seeking to go. What is the most valuable thing that you have? Of course, this will vary from person to person, but before we move on with the more practical things, take a moment to consider these deeper thoughts.

When I first started trying to boost my productivity, I ignored all of these things, preferring to implement more concrete and clear tips and hacks. It worked for a while, but I kept sliding back and my productivity kept dropping. It was only when I focused on these aspects first that I made any real progress.

It might seem silly at first, but this is one of the most important things you can do- it is so worth it!

Chapter 4: Letting go: The art of doing one thing at a time

Now that we have gotten the core practice out of the way, it is time to focus on some practical aspects of productivity. One of the biggest thieves of time is multitasking. Most people will tell you that they are very talented at multitasking and that doing multiple things at once is a great way to get more done.

I am here to refute that claim. Doing multiple things at once is terrible for your productivity and is not an effective way to manage your time, or your projects. In fact, if you are looking to improve your productivity, then you need to consider the art of doing one thing at a time.

This can be very challenging for most people, and feels counter-productive. However, it is one of the best things you can do for yourself. It has taken me many years to figure out how to do one thing at a time, but it has been so very worth it!

I often have many projects on the go at the same time but, whenever possible, I try and complete them one at a time. I also shut off any other distractions while I am working. This is very helpful, as I am not being distracted by my emails every few minutes, and I am not getting distracted by a boiling-over stove.

But what about the days where you just can't avoid it? If you have children, for example, you might have to be running a bath while you answer an email. Trust me, I know how that feels, but there is a way to work around that!

Find a time during your day where you have uninterrupted time. Schedule your most important work for that block of time, and stick to your commitment. Get that done in your most productive time, and then move on to multitasking, if necessary.

When you need to multitask, do so with tasks that do not require big blocks of time or attention. This might include answering emails or doing administrative tasks, instead of doing your core work. This is a good way to find balance in your day and get the best of both worlds.

Learning to let go can be very challenging at first, but once you get the hang of it, your productivity will sky rocket and your stress will decrease substantially. In my personal opinion, this is a win-win situation.

Chapter 5: Start off your day right

Now that you have mastered the art of focusing on one thing at a time, the next step is to make sure that you start your morning off right. This is a very important aspect of having a productive day and it is something that most people neglect.

If I run out of the house, almost late, without having eaten breakfast, my coffee getting cold on my desk, then I can be certain my day just won't be that productive. At one stage in my life, this used to happen every day and I was constantly in a bad mood.

However, since I started focusing on my morning routine and trying to streamline it, things have started getting a lot easier for me. Streamlining your morning routine and starting your day off right can take some planning and work, at first, but once you have it organized the benefits will start rolling in.

A good way to start your day off right is to make sure to take care of as many tasks as possible the night before.

Make lunches, if that is something that you do, and make sure that clothes are ready and set out.

Set out your tasks for the next day and, if it is possible, make sure breakfast is ready to go. Try not to leave any big chores for the morning, and get them sorted in the evening. If you have children, then it is a good idea to make sure that homework is done and sorted, and that their bags are packed and ready to go.

These steps might seem obvious, but the stress and chaos that they save you in the morning will be worth it. Suddenly, most of your chores are taken care of and you only need to deal with getting yourself ready and into a productive mindset.

By freeing yourself of the mundane tasks, you have the opportunity to start getting your work done early, and, at the very least, your morning will be more peaceful and more streamlined, which sets you up for success no matter how you look at it.

If you can bare to get up early, then set your alarm clock for 10 minutes earlier than usual and get up when it goes off. This gives you ten minutes of time that you wouldn't usually have and can help you breathe settle and get the most out of the day. Remember, your mornings are the time to prime your body, mind and soul for success!

Chapter 6: 30 minutes morning ritual to bulldoze your day

So, by now you've made sure to relegate your chores to the evening before hand and you find yourself with more time in the morning. How should you use this time to benefit yourself, increase your productivity and set yourself up for success and not failure?

Well, we've got you covered! In this chapter, I have included a 30 minute plan to set yourself up for success in a big way. Of course, you might have to tailor this to your own family, but if you can get most of this done, then you'll be ready for success!

<u>Have a glass of water (2 minutes)</u>

When you first wake up, get out of bed and pour yourself a glass of water. You can add lemon if you like- have it hot or cold, depending on your preference.

Drinking water when you get up helps you wake up, improves energy, circulation and health. Basically, it is the best way to start your day, so make sure you have that glass of water the moment your feet hit the floor!

Stretch (3 minutes)

Now, most of us don't have time to exercise in the morning, but taking time to stretch and wake up your muscles is a great way to get yourself into a productive mindset. Besides, you cannot take care of your mind and neglect your body. Productivity is a combination of all these things, so it is important to be aware of your body!

Shower (10 minutes)

This is your time to shower, get dressed and feel fresh about the day. Some people opt for cold showers in the morning to instil resolve in themselves, and ensure that they are awake, refreshed and ready.

This, of course, is optional. Feel free to have either a hot shower or a cold shower, whatever appeals to you. Get ready like you usually do, getting dressed and ready for the day.

Affirmations (1 minute)

Take the time to repeat some simple affirmations in the mirror before you leave the bathroom. This doesn't have to take long at all, but the process of repeating these affirmations can have a big impact on your mindset, on your productivity and how the rest of your day goes.

Breakfast (10 minutes)

Breakfast is often overlooked, but assemble yourself a healthy breakfast that has sustainable energy in it. Choices include eggs, oats, yogurt and fruit. Whole grain toast is another effective breakfast. Make sure your breakfast is filling and wholesome and you'll be off to a great start!

Review your day (4 minutes)

While you eat your breakfast, go over your notes for the day ahead. Make sure you know what your goals are for the day, what you hope to achieve and any important appointments that you need to keep and be aware of.

This thirty-minute routine might not sound like much, but it allows you to take care of your body, your mind and your soul all at once, giving you the boost you need.

If you have other chores and responsibilities, feel free to work them in, but everyone should be able to find half an hour in their morning to take care of their own needs. I hope this helps you have many great mornings!

How to prime your mind, body and soul

Taking care of your mind, body and soul is imperative to making sure you have a productive day. You can achieve this by making sure you follow the above thirty minute routine, and focus on having a good breakfast, hydration and adequate time to stretch your body and prepare for your day.

Ensuring that you engage in positive, daily affirmations and review your day before you get started is also a fantastic way to prepare your mind and prime it for success. If you want to succeed, you need to make sure that you are prepared for the work, prepared for your tasks and ready to start right away. One way to do this is by asking yourselves a set of questions during your daily review. Consider these questions honestly and you will be rewarded by clear focus and concise plan of attack for the day.

3 questions highly productive people ask themselves every day

1. What are my three most important tasks for the day?

Successful people know what their top three tasks are for the day. This helps them avoid getting side tracked. They know what they need to achieve today and they are better equipped to make it happen. This removes wasted time wondering what to focus on.

2. What major commitments and appointments do I have?

Productive people know what commitments and appointments they have. This allows them to honor their commitments, but avoid being controlled by them. Instead of getting side tracked, they are prepared to tackle each commitment as it comes and they are ready with any paper work that they require. This eliminates any extra stress and allows for a calm and collected approach to life.

3. What is my over-all goal and how will my tasks help me achieve it?

Productive people make sure that they keep the greater goal in mind. They keep their why at the front of their mind and assess how every task is getting them closer to this goal. If the task does not further their goal, they do not devote as much attention and time to it. If the task if valuable towards their goal, then they allow this knowledge to motivate them and ensure that they are focused on the task at hand.

Asking yourself these questions every day is a very powerful way to center yourself and be assured that you are on the way to achieving your goals. It is also very motivating and helps you prime your mind and your soul for success that day.

Practice daily affirmation

Daily affirmations are a great tool to improve productivity, mindset and get you on your way to having a very successful day. Once you have established your list of affirmations then they do not take long to implement at all. They should take you approximately 1 minute every morning, although you can repeat the affirmations throughout the day, as it suits you and as you require.

Before you start writing your affirmations, it is important to make sure you know what you want your affirmations to achieve. They need to be empowering and motivation, as well as uplifting. This means different things to different people, but focus on what phrases make you feel motivated and empowered and you can't go wrong.

It can be worth writing a list of affirmations, just to make sure you are ready to go every morning. You can use the same affirmation every day, if you like, or you can change it up depending on what you need that day and what your commitments are.

Below, we have included a worksheet to make it easier for you to decide on your affirmations, and assist you in compiling a comprehensive list of affirmations.

Affirmation Worksheet 1

In this worksheet we will evaluate your goals, what you want to achieve with your affirmations and what sort of uplifting things you would like to hear. Answer these as honestly as possible and with as much detail as you can. Remember, honesty is key here and it doesn't matter if it takes a little while to get through this list.

It is important that the affirmations you use are tailored to you and your needs so that they have a great impact on your life and on your mornings!

What are your goals?

_____

_____

_____

_____

What inspires you to be your best self?

_____

_____

What would you like to achieve with your affirmations?

What type of things would you say to a friend to uplift them?

What type of things do you like to hear when you need a boost?

What puts you in a good mood?

_____

_____

_____

_____

Now that you have a good idea of what makes you tick, we will move onto the next worksheet and start writing the actual affirmations! This can get a bit tricky, but you're already put in the hard work in this worksheet, and it's about to pay off.

Affirmation Worksheet 2

In this worksheet, we will be focusing on discovering which words you find most uplifting and empowering and putting them together in phrases. Feel free to refer to your previous worksheet if you need any help. And remember, have fun and be true to yourself!

<u>Write a list of positive words</u>

_____
_____
_____
_____

<u>Write a list of powerful words</u>

_____
_____
_____
_____

<u>Write a list of empowering phrases</u>

_____
_____

Write a list of affirmations using these words and phrases

Write 5 affirmations for when you are stressed

Write 5 affirmations for when things are going well

Write 5 affirmations for when things are not going well

_____
_____
_____
_____

Write 5 affirmations that motivate you

_____
_____
_____
_____

Write 5 affirmations that make you smile

_____
_____
_____
_____

Write 5 affirmations that empower you

_____

_____

_____

_____

Now that you have worked your way through the list, you probably have a lot of great material, so remember that these affirmations are there for you to use whenever you need them! Use them freely and with abandon.

Now, you probably have a great list of affirmations that you can use when you are in a number of different situations, but just in case you need some more, I have included a list of affirmations that I personally use to get through the daily grind and stay productive. Enjoy!

1. I am powerful and I will make the life that I want a reality.

2. I love, I live and I am excited about the day.

3. I am the one in charge of my mind.

4. I have a strong body, a strong mind and a strong spirit.

5. I believe that everything will work out for the best.

6. I am special and I feel good about being myself.

7. I believe that amazing opportunities are presenting themselves.

8. I am calm, I am in control and I am getting things done.

9. I know what I need to do and I will make a positive contribution.

10. I am in control; I lead my own life.

11. I believe that good things are just around the corner.

12. I will make the choice to be happy and to love and enjoy my life.

13. I will appreciate everything that I have and enjoy it all to the full.

14. I am productive and I am positive.

15. I choose to live my life to the fullest.

16. I am focused and I will work with purpose.

17. I am very thankful for each of my blessings and opportunities.

18. I am creating my own life and opportunities.

19. I can do anything that I set my mind to.

20. I have all the tools that I need to have a productive day.

Chapter 7: Avoid Winning lottery mindset

Now that your morning routine is sorted and you have a stack of great affirmations in your arsenal, you need to make sure that you stick to a focused mindset. In fact, your mindset can make or break your productivity and success.

One of the most detrimental mindsets is the "Winning the lottery" mindset. This mindset dictates that you sit around waiting for your 'big break', waiting for someone else to take care of your problems, waiting for the miracle cure that will fix everything for you.

If you follow this mindset, then you allow yourself to embrace the victim mentality, which is a terrible thing to start doing. It drains your energy and you waste your time lamenting what could have been, or what could be if you just get that big break that raise, that promotion, etc.

This is the enemy of productivity. Productivity and hard work will help you achieve success, not waiting around for something to fix all your problems and answer your prayers. It is very important to keep this in mind when you start working on your productivity. Kill the lottery mindset and step forward into success!

Chapter 8: The need for a break in-between work day

In the quest for productivity, too many people feel like they cannot afford to take a break, and cannot afford to slow down at any point. This is a terrible mentality, as all it does is burn you out completely.

Productive people know that breaks are necessary for effective function and they pay close attention to the needs of their bodies and minds. If you are exhausted and pushing yourself to the brink of burn out then you productivity will not be sustainable. Instead of working non-stop and burning out, you need to take scheduled breaks.

The easiest way to do this is by using the Pomodoro technique. This technique involves working for 25 minutes, and then taking a four minute break.

This needs to be repeated four times, before a longer break (approximately 30 minutes) is taken. This is a fantastic way to work in breaks and still maintain your productivity. It is a technique I personally use all the time, especially when writing and I can vouch for it- it really helps me stay on track and get things done.

It is especially helpful if you are struggling to get started on a task.

Committing to 25 minutes of work is easier than committing to several hours' worth of work. It also allows you to give your mind a bit of a breather and gives you time to stretch your body, especially if you are doing desk work.

While this technique won't work for everyone, it is a very helpful guideline for success.

Chapter 9: Deadline is not your enemy but your best friend

When most people hear the word deadline, they immediately experience a sense of dread and exhaustion. Deadlines are often associated with a sense of stress, worry and late nights trying to get things finished in time.

That said, a deadline is really not that bad. In fact, a deadline is often the thing that motivates us to get things finished and stay productive. In fact, deadlines have motivated people for many years and I bet that you have accomplished huge amounts of work when trying to beat a deadline!

A great way to take advantage of this is to set yourself personal deadlines. Decide to have a project completed by a certain time or day, and stick to it! Enforce deadlines on yourself that are, hopefully, before your actual deadline. This gives you time to review the work in an effective way and make sure that your quality is always up to standard.

If you work for yourself, set up some form of accountability, like a partner or a friend who has similar deadlines, or post a launch date for your project online and make it public. It is important to make sure you are accountable and that you will really hit the deadline that you set for yourself.

This sense of urgency can be used to drive you on and help you complete your work and your tasks. So next time you badmouth a deadline, stop and consider that when it comes to productivity, it might just be your best friend!

Chapter 10: How to protect your time

Most of us are, by heart, people pleasers. We don't like saying no to other people, in case it upsets them or offends them in some way. We want to be seen as nice, helpful and motivated. We don't want to say no to a project in case our boss thinks that we can't handle our jobs.

We want to say yes to everything, but this often comes at the cost of our sanity and time. Time is your most valuable asset and you must learn to protect it. Start by learning to say no to things. Don't agree to every project, invitation or suggestion that comes your way.

It is okay to say no. As difficult as it is at first, realize that other people will be okay if you say no. Honor your most important and vital commitments and let go of the rest- it will all work out in the end,

Block out appointments with yourself and make sure that you keep them.

Block off an hour to work on your core project and don't let anyone else bother you during this time. It is not selfish to put yourself first sometimes, and you will be doing yourself, and everyone else a favor. It is important to remember that people will respect your time commitments and constraints if you are clear about them.

Don't fall into the trap of saying yes to everything, stressing yourself out and getting nothing done. Protect your time my scheduling appointments with yourself and keeping them. You will be less stressed, more productive and better at what you do. This is a win-win for you and for everyone around you, so learn to say no!

Chapter 11: The secret to eliminate distractions

The secret to eliminating distractions is really simple when it comes down to it. It is important to make sure that you make a conscious effort to block out the time to work. This might seem like a small thing, but it can make all the difference.

Turning off your phone and making sure that your Facebook and email are shut down can be very difficult for a whole day. It can be tempting to check just that one thing and let your attention waver. Once you have done that it can be hard to get back on track again. This is often how we lose our productive streak and let things go downhill.

However, it is much easier to shut of your distractions for just one or two hours. You can commit to an hour or two and shut everything down for that time.

You can make sure you don't schedule any appointments at this time.

You can get up early before anyone else is awake. Whatever it is you need to do to make it work, the key thing, the secret to success, is to make sure that you make a conscious effort to block out time for work. It might not seem like much, but it really can make or break your productivity, and it is most definitely worth a try. I can almost guarantee that you will like it! You can use social media and email checking as mini "breaks" if you like, but make sure that you set timers for them too, so that you don't stay on break for too long!

Chapter 12: Productivity hacks

a.   Turn off all alerts

This might seem like a no brainer, but turning off all of your phone, email and social media alerts is such a time saver! There is nothing wrong with checking alerts during your work day- sometimes you are waiting for an important email, and so it can be so tempting to keep your alerts on. However, it is very important that you focus on work while you are working, and check alerts at a designated time.

This might seem hard, but if you have been working for 25 minutes solid, set a 5 minute timer and spend the time checking social media and getting a drink of water. You don't have the constant interruptions of leaving alerts on, but you still have the opportunity to check everything, and in a more relaxed and enjoyable fashion.

It also removes the guilt, so you'll feel less stressed, less worried and more settled throughout your work day. For me, I find that this is a huge plus! For me, emails are hard to avoid, while I don't check social media very often. I will say that turning off alerts has stopped me from constantly interrupting my flow to check the latest spam that has floated into my inbox, so I personally recommend this hack quite highly.

The important thing here is to tailor it to suit your personal needs and feelings. If you can do this, I am sure that you will have great success.

b.   Ignore the news

We live in an age of constant information, and this is the same for the news. We are constantly bombarded by twitter feeds, articles and emails that are updated constantly. There is an almost endless stream of news and a lot of it can be very distressing.

Much like turning off your alerts, it is important to avoid getting sucked into the news. While it is important to be up to date on current events, it is not ideal to do it during the middle of your work day.

It is very easy to grow distressed and distracted by bad news, and it is easy to get sucked into the endless stream of information as you check for updates. It is easy to get caught up in this and I have done it myself many times, finding myself checking the news on an almost hourly basis if the story concerns me.

Unfortunately, though, this does you no favors when it comes to your productivity. In fact, this can slow your productivity down substantially, so it is important to turn off your news updates and leave them off until the end of your day. It is worth noting, though, that keeping on fire or flood alerts is always a smart idea, if you live in an area that is very prone to these sorts of problems. That said, unless there is a threat of a major emergency, it is wise to keep your news feed updates to a minimum.

c. Limit your meetings to 30 minutes per day

If you are used to working in an office, then you are probably used to having several meetings every day, or one long one that drains everyone's time and energy and gets very little done.

If you are looking to improve your productivity then you need to do your best to break this habit and break it fast. It is important to consider the purpose of a meeting before you attend it.

Write out your questions and what you want to accomplish beforehand, as well as suggestions and other ways to streamline the meeting. If you are in control of your time, make sure everyone knows to do the same, and schedule concise meetings with only people you definitely have to talk to.

This is a great way to cut back on your wasted time, while still getting things done with your team. As a rule, try and stick to approximately 30 minutes of meetings during your day, less if you can get away with it.

It might seem impossible, but once you start arriving to your meetings with everything ready to go and laid out, as well as a concise idea of what you want to discuss, things will become easier. Also, if you can talk about it via email (and it won't take up more time!) then that is also a good option.

I have personally never been a fan of meetings, so I avoid them whenever possible. When that's not an option though, arm yourself and get in and out as quickly as possible. The time it saves you is amazing!

d.   Make the most of your hours

Whenever possible, try and make the most of all of your time. This might seem obvious, but it is easy to overlook all of your wasted time. If, instead of wasting it, you could harness it into productivity, then chances are you could have more leisure hours, or time to focus on other important things.

A good example of this is your commute. If you can use this time to make phone calls (If you do not drive), or listen to an audiobook (if you do drive), then you are immediately improving the way you spend your time.

Another way to harness your hours is to consider outsourcing some of your chores and responsibilities. For example, can you order your groceries online and pick them up at the store, instead of doing a whole shop yourself? This would save you time and probably have you eating healthier (I know I always throw extra things into my cart!).

Could you hire someone to do your taxes, or to help you clean the house? This will be different depending on who you are and what your chores and responsibilities are, but consider outsourcing if you can. It helps reduce stress, reduce your responsibilities and free up your time so that you can truly make the best of all your hours, instead of wasting your time.

Of course, this will differ for each person, but try and identify your wasted hours and how you can save time. I'm sure there's more time in your day than you realized!

e. Zoom into your to-do's

Another way to stay productive is to focus on your most important task for the day. I advocate choosing your three most important tasks for the day, and then picking your number 1. This is the task that you will complete first.

Schedule time to complete this task and make it clear that you cannot be disturbed. Make sure that your calendar is not open for this block of time and that you alerts are all off. If you can close your door, do so too.

Defintely, it is important to schedule all three tasks into your day, but making one task an absolute priority will help you stay on track, no matter what else comes up in your day. Even if your day falls apart from that point on, you will know that you achieved one of your goals and are closer to your ultimate goal.

This might seem simple, and it might seem counterproductive to focus on only a few things, but if they are core, important things for your work, then this is the best thing you can do for your productivity.

Protect your scheduled time and treat it like an appointment with your boss or a serious client. Make sure that you honor that commitment first, before you check emails or do anything else. This sets the rest of your day up for productivity. Also, as another tip, if you can schedule it for your most productive time, that is always an extra boost.

f. Declutter your work desk and room

If you are living with mess and chaos all the time, then your mind will most likely be in the same state. When everything around you is a mess, it is hard to know where to find things. Your productivity suffers as you search for the important document that you lost, or as you search for a pen to jot down some details.

A messy desk and a messy room make it impossible to stay effectively productive. Even if you have bursts of productiveness, in the long run, you will lose time and motivation.

On a personal note, I cannot handle a messy desk. My motivation sinks and I have no energy to do even the most basic tasks anymore. It is a real challenge and I hate having to deal with a messy work area.

A good way to remedy this is to set aside some time and do a big declutter. Throw out anything that you do not need and file the rest away. Get containers and holders to make sure the area stays neat and make sure you have a system in place to keep it that way.

Every day, clear your desk surface, and every week, do a bit of a clean through your draws and files. If you keep this up, you will never have to worry about a messy desk or room again and your productivity and mental health with most definitely thank you for it!

g.   Pay attention to temperature

Most people believe that a cold environment will be a productive one, but that is not the case. It is true that too much warmth saps your productivity and focus, but the optimal temperature for focus is actually quite a comfortable one. Through many different studies, we have found that the ideal temperature for productivity is between 70 and 77 degrees Fahrenheit. The optimal temperature is exactly 71 degrees for most people, although everyone has their own, personal preferences.

If possible, set the thermostat to this temperature. This helps you feel energized, awake and focused. Be careful not to make it too warm, or you will feel sluggish. If the temperature is too cold, you will be distracted.

Most people do not even consider temperature that much when they consider productivity, but our environment is important and has a big impact on how well we work, how much we get done and how high the quality of the work is.

If you have no control over the temperature of your environment, then try and make sure you dress for optimal temperature. If your office is hot, dress in a cooler style, or buy a small desk fan. If your office is too cold, layer up and enjoy a more comfortable internal temperature.

Just remember, optimal temperature is that state where you don't really notice the temperature at all-because it is just right and you are feeling perfectly comfortable and at ease. Not a bad place to be!

h. Use your breaks wisely

When you are working hard, it can be tempting to take long breaks, or frequent breaks. However, it is important to use your breaks wisely and not just take them whenever you feel like it. Studies have found that breaks are most effective when they come after a solid block of work, and when they are short. A five minute break is effective, and you can have several short breaks like this through the day.

Once you have had several beaks of this length, you can take a longer, half an hour break. Studies don't recommend taking a longer break as this can interrupt your flow and make it difficult to get back into the flow of working.

After all, if you can get your work done sooner, you'll have the rest of the day off, so limiting your breaks and using them wisely can be a very helpful thing in the long run, both for your productivity and for your social life!

If you absolutely have to take a break right away, set a timer and get up to stretch. Try and do something different and engaging, like going for a walk, making a cup of tea or doing some long stretches and deep breathing. Getting up from your chair is always a good idea as it gets the blood flowing and helps you feel like you've actually had a break!

When the timer goes off, try and get back to work right away. This helps you stay in flow and achieve more. And after all, productivity is the name of the game.

i.   Use the pomodoro technique for time slots

This is something that we touched one earlier in the book and in the previous hack, but it is one of the greatest productivity tools out there, so we just had to mention it again.

The pomodoro technique is great for making sure you stay on track without feeling too burnt out. In fact, it is the optimal amount of work, with a perfect break ratio in between. This technique involves working for 25 minutes, and then taking a four minute break.

This needs to be repeated four times, before a longer break (approximately 30 minutes) is taken. This is a fantastic way to work in breaks and still maintain your productivity. It is a technique I personally use all the time, especially when writing and I can vouch for it- it really helps me stay on track and get things done.

It is especially helpful if you are struggling to get started on a task. Committing to 25 minutes of work is easier than committing to several hours' worth of work. It also allows you to give your mind a bit of a breather and gives you time to stretch your body, especially if you are doing desk work.

So next time you feel like you are in a rut, set a 25 minute timer and just start working. I guarantee that by the end of it, you will be back in the game and after a 5 minute break, you'll feel refreshed again and ready to keep going.

j.   Learn to say no

This is another topic that we touched on earlier, but learning to say no is absolutely vital to being productive and making real, lasting contributions to your work load and productivity.

That said, it can be so, so hard to say no to anything. After all, we want to be seen as nice, helpful and motivated. We don't want to say no to a project in case our boss thinks that we can't handle our jobs.

We want to say yes to everything, but this often comes at the cost of our sanity and time. Time is your most valuable asset and you must learn to protect it. Start by learning to say no to things. Don't agree to every project, invitation or suggestion that comes your way.

It is okay to say no. As difficult as it is at first, realize that other people will be okay if you say no. Honor your most important and vital commitments and let go of the rest- it will all work out in the end.

Block out appointments with yourself and make sure that you keep them. Block off an hour to work on your core project and don't let anyone else bother you during this time. It is important to remember that people will respect your time commitments and constraints if you are clear about them.

Don't fall into the trap of saying yes to everything, stressing yourself out and getting nothing done. Protect your time my scheduling appointments with yourself and keeping them. You will be less stressed, more productive and better at what you do.

k.   Wake up earlier

If you can only mange to wake up 10 minutes earlier than usual, that is still 10 minutes that you did not have before. If you can wake up half an hour earlier, than you can fit a huge chunk of your morning routine in before you would usually be awake!

Many productive people swear by waking up earlier, and so many successful people can't be wrong! By waking up earlier, you set yourself up for success and you are already ahead of the game and the

competition. Not only that, it you will most likely find yourself feeling more energized, more accomplished and more settled before you even step a foot out of the door. That, alone, is worth a few minutes of lost sleep! That said, it doesn't have to be lost sleep if you go to bed a little earlier.

Now, it might not seem like that big a deal, sleeping earlier and getting up earlier. You have the same amount of time awake, so it shouldn't be a big deal And yet, it is. People have reported feeling more productive when they get up earlier, and that feeling carries them through the day, improving performance and productiveness, as well as mood, throughout the whole day. Give it and try and beat your alarm clock once and for all! (We all push the snooze button too often, anyway- myself definitely included in this.)

1. Go to bed at a regular hour

We touched on this before, but it is hard to get up early if you are staying up late! Try and go to bed at a regular hour, and make it a decent hour too. For example, going to bed at 9pm one night and 12pm another just confuses your body and makes it difficult for you to get a good sleep.

However, if you consistently to go bed at 10pm-11pm, your body knows what to expect and it can act accordingly. This helps prime your body for better rest and assist you in getting the most from your sleep.

Now, of course, this doesn't mean that you can't have the occasional night out or sleep in in the mornings. As long as your average sleeping pattern is a regular one, then you will be just fine. It is all about training your body to know when to expect sleep, and helping it get that sleep in a regular manner.

It seems like a simple thing, but it can make the absolute world of difference when it comes to your health and your productivity. It helps you work with a clearer head, in helps regulate your health, your weight and your mood and it will improve these things over time, as long as you remain consistent.

You'll find yourself working better and more productively and craving less snack foods and caffeine. This is beneficial to your short term and long term health and career goals, so it is worth taking on board.

m.   Eat healthily

This might seem unrelated to productivity, but hear me out! If you are eating nothing bug processed carbs and sugar, then you will experience significant sugar crashes and drops in your energy levels. If you are skipping breakfast and loading up on caffeine, then your energy won't be sustainable and your productivity will drop.

Maintaining a healthy body and healthy sugar levels go a long way with ensuring that your body is able to maintain steady energy levels. If your energy levels are stable, then your productivity levels remain stable too.

It all starts by having a good breakfast rich with complex carbohydrates, protein and sustainable food, such as oats, eggs and fruit.

Regular, healthy snacks through the day will help you to maintain your energy levels. Stay away from a heavy lunch, but make sure you still have one that is filling so that you are not left hungry. Stay hydrated with plenty of water throughout the day and you will find that your energy levels remain consistent and your health improves too!

After all, everything is connected and your body and brain have to work together to keep you healthy and productive. If you take care of your body it will help you achieve your goals and maintain your productive lifestyle. Body, mind and soul are always connected and by taking good care of them all, you will find you reach success much easier than you thought possible.

n. Be accountable

Accountability is a tried and tested way to make sure you get the motivation and extra push that you need to achieve your goals, so always keep it in mind when embarking on a project or task.

Accountability is very useful. Without it, we have no real need to complete a task. If you work for yourself, or even if you work for a company, it can be very helpful to set yourself personal deadlines. Decide to have a project completed by a certain time or day, and stick to it! Enforce deadlines on yourself that are, hopefully, before your actual deadline. This gives you time to review the work in an effective way and make sure that your quality is always up to standard.

If you work for yourself, set up some form of accountability, like a partner or a friend who has similar deadlines, or post a launch date for your project online and make it public. It is important to make sure you are accountable and that you will really hit the deadline that you set for yourself. This sense of urgency can be used to drive you on and help you complete your work and your tasks. Accountability can work wonders, so next time you find yourself in a rut, set up a deadline and get some accountability. Even if this is as simple as telling a friend about it. Every little bit helps and you will reach your goal before you know it, with just a little nudge from a friend!

Chapter 13: Identifying, sand removing your destructive habits

One of the problems with improving your productivity is that you have to over -hall your habits in a big way. By this I mean that you need to try and focus not only on adding positive habits, but you also need to focus on eliminating your destructive habits.

This can be tricky as we often are not aware that we are engaging in these sorts of habits, or what they are costing us productivity wise. These habits can include: saying yes to everything, frequently checking social media, pushing the snooze button one time too many or relying too heavily on sugar and caffeine.

All of these habits might seem harmless at the time, but they will steal your productivity slowly and steadily until you are wondering where the heck the day just went, and why you haven't gotten anything done yet.

If you find yourself struggling with little habits that suck your time and productivity, then this is the chapter for you. It is time to have a good, hard look at what you are doing and how you can start to improve these habits.

The first thing to do is to start recording your day. Make notes about every interruption, every stop in your work flow, why you stopped and what you did. Continue with this, including keeping record of what you eat, etc. Try and do this for a few days if you can, to get an accurate picture of what you do every day. Now is not the time to try and pretty -it-up. Record things honestly or you'll never get a true reading of your situation, which will be detrimental to the practice of doing this. Once you have your detailed outline of your day, have a good hard think and answer the following questions:

1.   **Where do you find most of your time going?**

2.   **What is taking up the most of your rime (outside of work)?**

3.   **Do you have food habits you would like to change or work on?**

4. How do you think you can eliminate distractions and make the most of your time?

Once you have determined the areas that you want to work on, start tackling them one by one. If you have a problem with your social media usage, then try and app that blocks it for set amount of time and allows you to focus on your work.

If you want to eat healthier, try getting healthy but convenient meals, and work your way up gradually into a full, healthy diet. Start by making just one change, and continue on from there.

Identifying the problem is the most important part. Once you're aware of it and ready to work on it, you're already half way there. Start small and slow, keep your why in mind always, and ensure that you keep the end goal in mind.

You can do it. You can overcome your problems one step at a time and you can achieve the success that you dream of. Remember, you just need to start and then keep going.

Chapter 14: Using your time to your advantage (make it your leverage, not just average!)

Time is a fantastic thing. You have 24 hours every day to work on your goals, dreams, to do lists and leisure time. To many people, time is just another thing to quantify. Everyone has time, so why is it so special?

For most people, time is a very average thing that does not do much to help you further your goals or improve yourself. However, this couldn't be more wrong. In fact, if you use it right, time is a fantastic leverage that can help you achieve all of your wildest dreams.

Don't believe me? Well think about all of the hours you put into learning a new skill, for example. By using your time to learn something new, to learn and to grow, you have leveraged your time effectively, using it to catapult you into success.

The same can be said for time and for productivity. Your time is precious-every moment counts, so it is important to either spend your time being productive, or spend your time on something that you love. If you are particularly lucky, you can be productive and love your job too.

Leveraging your time is a very important skill to learn. A simple way to start is to ask yourself a few questions:

1.   How much time do I have to work on this project/ goal?

2.   How will I feel when I complete this goal?

3.   Can I find extra time to achieve it?

4.   How can I use my dead hours (time like commuting)

5.   How do I want my life to look?

By asking yourself these questions, you start focusing on what time is available to you and what you can achieve with it.

So what makes time so special? Well, time is what allows you to live, to breathe, and to complete your tasks. Not only that, but we are all aware that our time is limited.

This can be one of the most powerful motivators. It has motivated people through history and it can motivate you. We only have a limited amount of time- our time is not infinite nor should we expect it to be.

Our time is limited, so we need to choose what we do with it wisely . We need to make sure that we spend our time in a way that makes us proud. If you want to achieve something, then you need to start now, not later.

Our time is limited and we never know how limited. So think about your why, think about what motivates you and what drives you and let time be your best leverage. Let time be your best motivator. Work like your future depends on it, because it just might.

You have what it takes to succeed and you have all of the tools you require at your disposal. You can achieve it- you can overcome procrastination and achieve your goals.

Chapter 15: Conclusion

Congratulations for making it this far! To have made your way through this type of book is impressive. If you've been implementing the advice, then that is even more inspiring. If not, don't forget to go back through the book later (as soon as possible), and start putting it all into practice.

Reading it won't help unless you actively put it into practice, but I am sure that you already know that. After all, most of this book has been focused on putting your thoughts into action, so I hope that it has given you a few good ideas.

At the beginning of this book, I said that starting out is always the hardest part, especially when it comes to transforming your life. Starting might be the hardest part, but it is also the most important part. It brings with it momentum, inspiration, determination and a desire to achieve something.

I stand by that, and I believe that you have well and truly tackled the first step head on. You are closer to your dreams that you have ever been before. You just need to keep moving forward.

After all, those who never start never achieve anything, so take a moment to pat yourself on the back. You've done more than most people ever will in their lives-not only have you started, but you've made it to the end of the book and I know you're just rearing to go and make some big changes! The tips and tricks in this book are not just meant to be read, but they are meant to be used and implemented to ensure that you reap the benefits.

In this book, we have touched on many things. We have talked about creating an ideal environment for work, through removing distractions and clutter. We have talked about keeping things at an optimal temperature and we have talked about shutting down alerts and other distractions, such as the news.

We have highlighted the importance of learning to say no and to blocking out your time. We have also gone through some handy techniques for blocking out time for yourself, so that you take effective breaks and get the work done that you need to. This cannot be underestimated. Breaks are very important and I hope that we have highlighted that for you in this book.

We also discussed the importance of starting your day off right, by priming your body, your mind and yours soul. This includes having a good breakfast and plenty of time to get everything done. You can free up time by getting up earlier, or by doing some chores the night before.

Probably most important in the morning routine is the process of laying out your three most important tasks for the day, and working through your goals for the day. The affirmations are quite valuable too, as these can uplift you when you are going through a difficult time, or if you just need a bit of an extra book.

Round it off with a good breakfast and a calm morning and you have a perfect start to your day. Walking out of the door calmly instead of skidding out, almost late for work and having barely had a cup of coffee for breakfast is not a sustainable way to live and will cause significant mood drops and problems in productivity later on.

We also talked about why it is so important to make sure you are accountable and that you will really hit the deadline that you set for yourself. Deadlines are fantastic for this and they can help create a sense of urgency can be used to drive you on and help you complete your work and your task. If you take responsibility for your actions, your time and your deadlines you will achieve far greater success than the person who sits around waiting for their big break.

Remember, you are your big break. You are the reason for your own success and hard work and dedication can take you anywhere. Do not forget this, especially when you are having a hard time. This is not a bad this- this is empowering. If you are responsible for your own life, then you have the power to change your life, the power to grow and develop and improve yourself every single day. You have this power and you have full control over your own life.

Commitment, determination and motivation are fantastic tools to making sure that you achieve what you have set out to do. After all, this book has laid all out for you, so all you need to do is work through the book's instructions and you will find the success you crave.

Sometimes, though, that isn't enough just to follow the rulebook. In this case, what you need, what you truly need, is to believe in yourself and in your dreams. Hold onto your why, hold onto the thing that drives you and motivates you and you can do anything. Hold onto the reasons for your hard work, hold onto the reasons for your career, your plans, and your studies.

Hold on and keep moving forward no matter what. Remember that you hold the power to change your own life and you hold the power to succeed. For every mistake that knocks you to your knees, there is a great success waiting for you.

These tips and tricks might take a while to get used to. They might take a week or a month to get your head around, so don't give up if they don't work on the very first try. Keep at it, keep practicing and keep trying. It won't be long until you find the success you deserve. You have already taken the first step to greatness.

The important thing now, is to not stop. After all, you can do anything.

www.ingramcontent.com/pod-product-compliance
Lightning Source LLC
Chambersburg PA
CBHW050232230526
45470CB00005B/1909